~A BINGO BOOK~

Colonial America Bingo Book

COMPLETE BINGO GAME IN A BOOK

Written By Rebecca Stark

ISBN 978-0-87386-455-8

Educational Books 'n' Bingo

Printed in the U.S.A.

ADDITION BINGO DIRECTIONS

INCLUDED:

List of Terms

Templates for Additional Terms and Clues

2 Clues per Term

30 Unique Bingo Cards

Markers

1. **Either cut apart the book or make copies of ALL the sheets. You might want to make an extra copy of the clue sheets to use for introduction and review. Keep the sheets in an envelope for easy reuse.**

2. Cut apart the call cards with terms and clues.

3. Pass out one bingo card per student. There are enough for a class of 30.

4. Pass out markers. You may cut apart the markers included in this book or use any other small items of your choice.

5. Decide whether or not you will require the entire card to be filled. Requiring the entire card to be filled provides a better review. However, if you have a short time to fill, you may prefer to have them do the just the border or some other format. Tell the class before you begin what is required.

6. There are 50 terms. Read the list before you begin. If there are any terms that have not been covered in class, you may want to read to the students the term and clues before you begin.

7. There is a blank space in the middle of each card. You can instruct the students to use it as a free space or you can write in answers to cover terms not included. Of course, in this case you would create your own clues. (Templates provided.)

8. Shuffle the cards and place them in a pile. Two or three clues are provided for each term. If you plan to play the game with the same group more than once, you might want to choose a different clue for each game. If not, you may choose to use more than one clue.

9. Be sure to keep the cards you have used for the present game in a separate pile. When a student calls, "Bingo," he or she will have to verify that the correct answers are on his or her card AND that the markers were placed in response to the proper questions. Pull out the cards that are on the student's card keeping them in the order they were used in the game. Read each clue as it was given and ask the student to identify the correct answer from his or her card.

10. If the student has the correct answers on the card AND has shown that they were marked in response to the *correct questions,* then that student is the winner and the game is over. If the student does not have the correct answers on the card OR he or she marked the answers in response to *the wrong questions,* then the game continues until there is a proper winner.

11. If you want to play again, reshuffle the cards and begin again.

Have fun!

TERMS

apothecary

apprentice

blacksmith

Boston Massacre

Boston Tea Party

candles

clothing

card

committee(s) of correspondence

cooper

craft

Declaration of Independence

First Continental Congress

foundry

Benjamin Franklin

French and Indian War

Patrick Henry

hornbook

Intolerable Acts

Jamestown

journeyman

Middle Colonies

milliner

Navigation Act

New Amsterdam

New England Colonies

Peter Minuit

Thomas Paine

William Penn

Philadelphia

Pilgrims

Plantation

Printer

Quakers

Quartering Act

St. Augustine

Salem

silversmith

slavery

Sons of Liberty

Southern Colonies

spinning

Squanto

Stamp Act

taxation

weaving

wheelwright

Roger Williams

Williamsburg

Peter Zenger

Additional Terms

Choose as many Colonial America term,s as you would like and write them in the squares. Repeat each as desired. Cut out the squares and randomly distribute them to the class. Instruct the students to place the square on the center space of their card.

Colonial America Bingo

Clues for Additional Terms

Write two or three clues for each of your Colonial America terms.

_____ 1. 2. 3.	_____ 1. 2. 3.
_____ 1. 2. 3.	_____ 1. 2. 3.
_____ 1. 2. 3.	_____ 1. 2. 3.

Apothecary

1. In colonial times the ___ was more than just a druggist.

2. In colonial times the ___ was not just a druggist; he also provided medical treatment and prescribed medicine.

Apprentice

1. An ___ is someone who serves another for a set period of time in order to learn a trade.

2. The person who teaches an ___ is called a master.

Blacksmith

1. This craftsman made and repaired iron or steel objects.

2. He worked in a forge. Among his tools were anvils and hammers. One of his most important jobs was to make horseshoes.

Boston Massacre

1. On March 5, 1770, 5 colonists were killed by British soldiers. The event became known as the ___.

2. Crispus Attucks was among those killed in the ___.

Boston Tea Party

1. December 16, 1773, colonists threw crates of tea belonging to the British East India Company into Boston Harbor. The incident is called the ___.

2. The colonists dressed as Native Americans during this protest.

Candles

1. ___ were important as a source of light because oil was expensive.

2. Most ___ were made of tallow, or rendered animal fat. The women made them once a year, usually in the fall.

Clothing

1. Loose, informal robes, called banyans; tight-fitting breeches; and a cravat or other neck cloth were typical items of men's ___.

2. A petticoat, an informal gown called a Brunswick, and a cape were typical items of women's ___.

Card

1. It was a tool used to comb and clean wool or flax.

2. The purpose of a ___ was to separate the coarse parts of flax or wool to make it suitable for spinning.

Committee(s) of Correspondence

1. They were formed to communicate with those people in other colonies who shared the same views.

2. The first formal ___ was established in Boston in 1764. It was formed to rally opposition to the Currency Act.

Cooper

1. A ___ is a person who makes or repairs barrels and casks.

2. Complete this analogy:

basketmaker: basket :: ___ : barrel

Colonial America Bingo

© Barbara M. Peller

Craft

1. This is the general term for an occupation requiring special skills.

2. The colonies had people such as coopers, silversmiths and blacksmiths who were skilled at their ___.

Declaration of Independence

1. It announced that the 13 colonies now considered themselves 13 independent states. Its rough draft was written by Thomas Jefferson.

2. This statement was adopted by the Continental Congress on July 4, 1776.

First Continental Congress

1. All the colonies except Georgia sent delegates to this convention that met on September 5, 1774, in Philadelphia.

2. This convention was a reaction to the Coercive Acts, called the Intolerable Acts by the colonists.

Foundry

1. It is a place where metal is melted and poured into molds.

2. The men who worked in the ___ fashioned beautiful items out of molten brass, pewter and bronze.

Benjamin Franklin

1. He was a scientist, inventor, printer, and statesman. He published *Poor Richard's Almanack*.

2. This Philadelphian was Postmaster General under the Continental Congress from 1775 to 1776.

French and Indian War

1. It was actually part of a larger war between Britain and France known as the Seven Years' War.

2. It was ended by the Treaty of Paris in 1763. As a result, Britain's colonial empire grew.

Patrick Henry

1. This Patriot is known for his "Give me liberty, or give me death" speech.

2. He was a member of the Virginia House of Burgesses and introduced the Virginia Stamp Act Resolutions in reaction to the Stamp Act.

Hornbook

1. It was used in the education of young children.

2. A sheet with letters of the alphabet was mounted on bone, wood or leather and protected by a transparent sheet of horn.

Intolerable Acts

1. They were passed to punish Massachusetts for the Boston Tea Party. The British called them the Coercive Acts.

2. Among other things, they called for the closing of the port of Boston until restitution for the lost tea was made.

Jamestown

1. It was the first permanent British settlement in the New World.

2. This settlement was founded on May 14, 1607.

Journeyman	Middle Colonies
1. It is a skilled craftsman who works for wages. The term comes from the French words meaning "day man." 2. Someone who has completed an apprenticeship and now works for wages is called a ___.	1. The ___ comprise Delaware, Pennsylvania, New York, and New Jersey. 2. They were sometimes called the Bread Colonies because of their production of wheat and grain. It was originally part of New Netherlands.
Milliner	**Navigation Act**
1. The ___ made hats, shirts and other clothing and accessories. 2. The ___ was usually a woman. She sold the fabric to make the hats, aprons, shirts and other items as well as the items themselves.	1. The ___ of 1660 said only English or colonial ships could trade with the colonies. 2. The ___ of 1663 said the colonies could only produce commodities not produced in Britain. Cotton, sugar and tobacco could only be traded within the Empire.
New Amsterdam	**New England Colonies**
1. This Dutch colonial settlement later became New York City. 2. To secure the settlers' rights to this property, Peter Minuit made a deal with the Manhattan Indians.	1. The ___ comprise Rhode Island, Connecticut, Massachusetts, and New Hampshire. 2. An important reason for the founding of the ___ colonies was religious freedom.
Peter Minuit	**Thomas Paine**
1. He bought Manhattan Island from local Native Americans. 2. In 1626 he became director-general of New Netherland.	1. He was a revolutionary pamphleteer. 2. He wrote the pamphlet *Common Sense* in which he advocated independence from Britain.
William Penn	**Philadelphia**
11. He was a Quaker, but he strove for religious freedom for everyone in Pennsylvania. 2. This founder of Pennsylvania signed a treaty with the Delaware (Leni Lenape) Indians.	1. The Liberty Bell summoned citizens of ___ to hear the first public reading of the Declaration of Independence. 2. The First Continental Congress met here in September 1774. The Second met here in May 1775.

Pilgrims

1. In 1620 this group of people set sail from Plymouth, England, on the *Mayflower*.

2. The ___ came for religious freedom. They signed an agreement called the Mayflower Compact.

Plantation

1. It is a large farm or estate.

2. The ___ system was important to southern agriculture beginning in the late 17th century.

Printer

1. The ___ was very important. He edited and published the newspapers. His shop often served as the post office.

2. The typical ___ usually had one or two common English presses and a variety of type fonts.

Quakers

1. The ___ came to Pennsylvania in 1656 for religious reasons.

2. William Penn was a ___; he founded Pennsylvania.

Quartering Act

1. The ___ of 1765 said soldiers could be housed in inns and taverns and unoccupied houses.

2. The ___ of 1774 said soldiers could be housed in occupied private homes as well as unoccupied ones and public places.

St. Augustine

1. It is the oldest continuously occupied European-established city in the continental United States.

2. This city was founded by the Spanish in 1565.

Salem

1. The "witch hunts" in this Massachusetts community began because some girls had convulsions and the doctor did not know why.

2. Nineteen people were hanged as a result of the witch trials here.

Silversmith

1. In Colonial days the ___ was almost like a sculptor. Paul Revere was one.

2. Among the things beautifully fashioned by the ___ were sterling coffee pots, teapots, and bowls.

Slavery

1. It is a practice in which people own other people.

2. ___ became important in the southern colonies because cultivation of tobacco was labor intensive.

Sons of Liberty

1. It was a secret organization of American Patriots.

2. Samuel Adams and Paul Revere were Massachusetts leaders of the secret organization known as the ___ .

Colonial America Bingo

© Barbara M. Peller

Southern Colonies 1. They comprised Maryland, Virginia, North Carolina, South Carolina, and Georgia. 2. The plantation system of agriculture was important in the ___.	**Spinning** 1. It is the art of twisting fibers together to form yarn. 2. A machine known as a ___ wheel was used to make yarn.
Squanto 1. ___ was introduced to the Pilgrims by Samoset. His real name was Tisquantum. 2. ___ helped the Pilgrims in several ways. He taught them how to fish and plant corn. He also acted as interpreter when necessary.	**Stamp Act** 1. Passed in 1765, this act imposed a tax on the colonists for every piece of printed paper they used. 2. Among the items taxed with this 1765 act were newspapers, legal documents, ship's papers, and playing cards.
Taxation 1. The colonists objected to the ___ resulting imposed by the Stamp Act and Sugar Act because their intent was to raise money, not to regulate commerce. 2. The colonists objected to ___ without representation.	**Weaving** 1. The art of ___ involved two sets of yarn, the warp and the weft. 2. In ___ the cloth is woven on a loom, a device to hold the warp threads.
Wheelwright 1. A ___ is someone who makes and repairs wooden wheels. 2. People with carriages depended upon the ___ for safe and relatively comfortable journeys.	**Roger Williams** 1. He was the founder of Rhode Island. 2. This founder of Rhode Island is best known for his advocacy of religious tolerance and for the separation of church and state.
Williamsburg 1. This settlement in Virginia was originally called Middle Plantation. 2. Middle Plantation was renamed ___ when the capital of Virginia moved here from Jamestown.	**Peter Zenger** 1. He was charged with libel when his newspaper criticized the British governor of New York. 2. He defended himself against the charge of libel by saying it isn't libel if it is true. He won.

Colonial America Bingo

© Barbara M. Peller

Colonial America Bingo

Navigation Act	Jamestown	Taxation	Williamsburg	Wheelwright
Committee(s) of Correspondence	Apothecary	Roger Williams	Printer	Milliner
Southern Colonies	Silversmith		New England Colonies	Quakers
Peter Zenger	Apprentice	Hornbook	Spinning	New Amsterdam
Peter Minuit	First Continental Congress	Cooper	Patrick Henry	Intolerable Acts

Colonial America Bingo

Peter Zenger	Squanto	Philadelphia	St. Augustine	Peter Minuit
New Amsterdam	Printer	Blacksmith	Apprentice	Sons of Liberty
Salem	First Continental Congress		Craft	Hornbook
Benjamin Franklin	Stamp Act	Silversmith	Thomas Paine	Milliner
Intolerable Acts	Roger Williams	Cooper	Committee(s) of Correspondence	Patrick Henry

Colonial America Bingo

Peter Zenger	Hornbook	Printer	Spinning	Southern Colonies
First Continental Congress	Apothecary	Clothing	Jamestown	Middle Colonies
Apprentice	Roger Williams		Sons of Liberty	Boston Massacre
Silversmith	Salem	Peter Minuit	Benjamin Franklin	Philadelphia
Patrick Henry	Committee(s) of Correspondence	Cooper	Thomas Paine	Taxation

Colonial America Bingo

Silversmith	Sons of Liberty	Peter Minuit	Committee(s) of Correspondence	Taxation
Pilgrims	Blacksmith	Jamestown	St. Augustine	Southern Colonies
New England Colonies	Benjamin Franklin		Wheelwright	Williamsburg
Hornbook	Slavery	Roger Williams	Cooper	Clothing
Journeyman	Intolerable Acts	Plantation	Patrick Henry	Quakers

Colonial America Bingo

Intolerable Acts	Wheelwright	Apprentice	Blacksmith	Committee(s) of Correspondence
Pilgrims	Hornbook	Clothing	Craft	Apothecary
Squanto	Quakers		Declaration of Independence	Foundry
Milliner	Sons of Liberty	Navigation Act	Thomas Paine	Journeyman
Printer	Cooper	Slavery	Silversmith	New England Colonies

Colonial America Bingo: Card No. 5

Colonial America Bingo

Boston Massacre	Sons of Liberty	Philadelphia	Squanto	Quakers
Spinning	Apprentice	Journeyman	Jamestown	Southern Colonies
St. Augustine	Clothing		Blacksmith	Craft
Cooper	Peter Minuit	Thomas Paine	Plantation	New England Colonies
New Amsterdam	Hornbook	Navigation Act	Taxation	Slavery

© Barbara M. Peller

Colonial America Bingo

Navigation Act	Sons of Liberty	Foundry	Declaration of Independence	Printer
New Amsterdam	Taxation	First Continental Congress	Apothecary	Pilgrims
Philadelphia	Williamsburg		Craft	Boston Tea Party
Silversmith	Benjamin Franklin	Southern Colonies	Peter Zenger	Salem
Cooper	Committee(s) of Correspondence	Thomas Paine	Plantation	Boston Massacre

Colonial America Bingo

New England Colonies	Sons of Liberty	Card	Spinning	Boston Tea Party
Pilgrims	Squanto	St. Augustine	Quakers	Blacksmith
Southern Colonies	Quartering Act		Taxation	Wheelwright
Patrick Henry	Silversmith	Peter Zenger	Journeyman	Benjamin Franklin
Roger Williams	Cooper	Plantation	Apprentice	New Amsterdam

Colonial America Bingo

Craft	Printer	First Continental Congress	Southern Colonies	Quakers
Journeyman	Squanto	New England Colonies	Apprentice	Taxation
Middle Colonies	Navigation Act		Apothecary	Card
Boston Tea Party	Intolerable Acts	Peter Minuit	Declaration of Independence	Foundry
Benjamin Franklin	Thomas Paine	Clothing	Peter Zenger	Wheelwright

Colonial America Bingo

Peter Zenger	Spinning	Blacksmith	St. Augustine	Slavery
Quakers	Boston Tea Party	Jamestown	Apothecary	Taxation
Quartering Act	Sons of Liberty		Williamsburg	Salem
Peter Minuit	Milliner	Journeyman	Thomas Paine	Middle Colonies
Candles	New Amsterdam	Philadelphia	Intolerable Acts	New England Colonies

Colonial America Bingo

Boston Massacre	Sons of Liberty	Apprentice	Journeyman	New Amsterdam
Card	Middle Colonies	Declaration of Independence	Craft	Jamestown
Pilgrims	Squanto		Philadelphia	First Continental Congress
Candles	Southern Colonies	Thomas Paine	Committee(s) of Correspondence	Peter Zenger
Clothing	Cooper	Navigation Act	Plantation	Printer

Colonial America Bingo

Printer	Wheelwright	Middle Colonies	Spinning	Craft
First Continental Congress	Roger Williams	Squanto	Plantation	Apothecary
Navigation Act	Foundry		Quakers	St. Augustine
Cooper	Benjamin Franklin	Taxation	Peter Zenger	Pilgrims
Sons of Liberty	Card	Quartering Act	Clothing	Boston Tea Party

Colonial America Bingo

Candles	Wheelwright	Boston Massacre	Middle Colonies	Quakers
Squanto	Card	Sons of Liberty	Craft	Salem
Spinning	Blacksmith		First Continental Congress	Foundry
New England Colonies	Thomas Paine	Boston Tea Party	Quartering Act	Peter Zenger
Cooper	Milliner	Plantation	Navigation Act	Declaration of Independence

Colonial America Bingo

Committee(s) of Correspondence	Squanto	Apprentice	Thomas Paine	Candles
Boston Tea Party	Navigation Act	Middle Colonies	Apothecary	Sons of Liberty
Journeyman	Williamsburg		Philadelphia	Clothing
Milliner	Craft	Quartering Act	Blacksmith	Boston Massacre
Cooper	St. Augustine	Salem	New Amsterdam	New England Colonies

Colonial America Bingo

Declaration of Independence	Craft	Apprentice	Printer	Spinning
Boston Massacre	Philadelphia	Jamestown	Squanto	Journeyman
Quakers	Navigation Act		Southern Colonies	Taxation
Cooper	Middle Colonies	Card	Thomas Paine	Candles
New Amsterdam	Benjamin Franklin	Plantation	Slavery	First Continental Congress

Colonial America Bingo: Card No. 15

Colonial America Bingo

Blacksmith	Middle Colonies	Card	Slavery	Stamp Act
St. Augustine	Salem	Foundry	Pilgrims	Williamsburg
Candles	Wheelwright		Quakers	First Continental Congress
Silversmith	Boston Tea Party	Cooper	Declaration of Independence	Peter Zenger
Journeyman	William Penn	Plantation	Benjamin Franklin	Sons of Liberty

Colonial America Bingo: Card No. 16

Colonial America Bingo

Candles	Weaving	French and Indian War	Middle Colonies	Committee(s) of Correspondence
Declaration of Independence	Journeyman	Thomas Paine	Williamsburg	Foundry
Craft	Peter Zenger		William Penn	Card
Intolerable Acts	New Amsterdam	New England Colonies	Apprentice	Salem
Peter Minuit	Clothing	Printer	Spinning	Wheelwright

Colonial America Bingo

Slavery	Quartering Act	Boston Tea Party	Journeyman	St. Augustine
Sons of Liberty	Candles	Peter Minuit	Quakers	Clothing
Craft	Salem		French and Indian War	Taxation
Intolerable Acts	Jamestown	Thomas Paine	Peter Zenger	Philadelphia
William Penn	Middle Colonies	Apprentice	Weaving	Boston Massacre

Colonial America Bingo

Quakers	Boston Massacre	Middle Colonies	Card	Quartering Act
Declaration of Independence	Spinning	Taxation	Printer	Williamsburg
Weaving	Committee(s) of Correspondence		Apothecary	Slavery
Philadelphia	William Penn	Peter Minuit	Benjamin Franklin	French and Indian War
Southern Colonies	Stamp Act	New Amsterdam	New England Colonies	Plantation

Colonial America Bingo

Quartering Act	Weaving	Spinning	Middle Colonies	Apothecary
Blacksmith	First Continental Congress	Pilgrims	Peter Minuit	St. Augustine
Wheelwright	Foundry		Silversmith	Jamestown
Intolerable Acts	New England Colonies	Patrick Henry	Benjamin Franklin	William Penn
Hornbook	Roger Williams	Stamp Act	Peter Zenger	French and Indian War

Colonial America Bingo

Declaration of Independence	Boston Massacre	Pilgrims	Middle Colonies	Milliner
Wheelwright	French and Indian War	Boston Tea Party	Card	Navigation Act
Salem	New Amsterdam		Weaving	Apprentice
Peter Minuit	Printer	William Penn	Intolerable Acts	New England Colonies
Silversmith	Stamp Act	Plantation	Candles	Benjamin Franklin

Colonial America Bingo: Card No. 21

Colonial America Bingo

Southern Colonies	Philadelphia	French and Indian War	Squanto	Candles
St. Augustine	Spinning	Slavery	Card	Apothecary
Boston Tea Party	Williamsburg		Navigation Act	Foundry
William Penn	Intolerable Acts	Benjamin Franklin	Jamestown	Committee(s) of Correspondence
Stamp Act	Clothing	Weaving	Salem	Pilgrims

Colonial America Bingo

Blacksmith	Weaving	Printer	Squanto	Plantation
Boston Massacre	Quartering Act	New Amsterdam	Declaration of Independence	Jamestown
Philadelphia	Candles		Patrick Henry	Navigation Act
Salem	Stamp Act	William Penn	Clothing	Benjamin Franklin
Milliner	New England Colonies	Roger Williams	Peter Minuit	French and Indian War

Colonial America Bingo

Blacksmith	Candles	Committee(s) of Correspondence	Weaving	Card
Quakers	Plantation	Pilgrims	St. Augustine	Navigation Act
Foundry	Slavery		Quartering Act	Salem
Milliner	Patrick Henry	William Penn	Clothing	Wheelwright
Hornbook	Silversmith	Stamp Act	Spinning	Roger Williams

Colonial America Bingo

Silversmith	Pilgrims	Weaving	Apprentice	French and Indian War
Jamestown	Milliner	Declaration of Independence	Blacksmith	Apothecary
Wheelwright	Card		Patrick Henry	William Penn
Slavery	Intolerable Acts	Roger Williams	Stamp Act	Williamsburg
Plantation	Committee(s) of Correspondence	Boston Tea Party	Journeyman	Hornbook

Colonial America Bingo

French and Indian War	Weaving	Patrick Henry	St. Augustine	Slavery
Peter Minuit	Spinning	Card	Quartering Act	Blacksmith
Milliner	Philadelphia		Williamsburg	Silversmith
Candles	Squanto	Intolerable Acts	Stamp Act	William Penn
Foundry	Journeyman	Apprentice	Roger Williams	Hornbook

Colonial America Bingo

Patrick Henry	Boston Tea Party	Weaving	Quartering Act	First Continental Congress
Milliner	Philadelphia	Declaration of Independence	William Penn	Apothecary
Thomas Paine	Roger Williams		Stamp Act	Silversmith
Slavery	Boston Massacre	Pilgrims	Hornbook	Jamestown
Candles	Williamsburg	French and Indian War	Southern Colonies	Foundry

Colonial America Bingo: Card No. 27

Colonial America Bingo

Quakers	Quartering Act	Peter Zenger	Weaving	Boston Tea Party
First Continental Congress	French and Indian War	Patrick Henry	Peter Minuit	Williamsburg
Roger Williams	Salem		Slavery	St. Augustine
Foundry	Southern Colonies	New Amsterdam	Stamp Act	William Penn
Squanto	Craft	Candles	Hornbook	Milliner

Colonial America Bingo

French and Indian War	Quartering Act	Slavery	Declaration of Independence	Craft
Milliner	Peter Minuit	Pilgrims	Foundry	Southern Colonies
Wheelwright	Patrick Henry		Apothecary	Weaving
First Continental Congress	Intolerable Acts	Taxation	Stamp Act	William Penn
Blacksmith	Card	Hornbook	Boston Massacre	Roger Williams

Colonial America Bingo: Card No. 29

Colonial America Bingo

Committee(s) of Correspondence	Weaving	St. Augustine	Craft	William Penn
Jamestown	Taxation	Philadelphia	Williamsburg	Apothecary
Hornbook	Clothing		Foundry	Pilgrims
Milliner	Boston Massacre	Quartering Act	Stamp Act	Patrick Henry
Intolerable Acts	Printer	Roger Williams	French and Indian War	Slavery

Colonial America Bingo: Card No. 30